THE TRUTH

DANIEL ARTHUR ZAGAYA

authorHOUSE®

AuthorHouse™
1663 Liberty Drive, Suite 200
Bloomington, IN 47403
www.authorhouse.com
Phone: 1-800-839-8640

©2008 Daniel Arthur Zagaya. All rights reserved.

No part of this book may be reproduced, stored in a retrieval system, or transmitted by any means without the written permission of the author.

First published by AuthorHouse 1/30/2008

ISBN: 978-1-4343-5302-3 (sc)

Library of Congress Control Number: 2007909615

Printed in the United States of America
Bloomington, Indiana

This book is printed on acid-free paper.

Dedications

I wrote this book for my Greatest Teacher, Friend, and Psychiatrist... God.

Bless You, God, for writing this book through me and giving me the privilege of Knowing the Powerful Truth, and for teaching me how to use the Gifts already inside of Me.

Thank you, God, for allowing Me to Know What Is Magnificent through guiding me through what is not.

This Book would also not be possible if not for all of the following:

For my Parents, Tom and Nancy Zagaya: Whose Endless Compassion, Wisdom, Guidance, and immeasurable Unconditional Love has taught me to truly see God in All things. And, for my Sister, Julia Zagaya, who will achieve any greatness She chooses.

And, for the Spiritual guidance of Courtney Amber Byrne, Kenny and Keegan Kirby, Lauren McCauley, Marnee Baker, Mark Parsons, Brenda J. Daugherty, Daniel and Lee Dunlap, Judy Vaughn, Nick Stevens, The Gant Family, The Davis Family, The Donnell Family, especially Grey, Chaise Benton, The Minnichs, Jonathan Keeney, Asher and Billy Freeman, Nathan Goznell, Dustin Trukken, Joel Smih, The Humphreys, Treven Cannon, Jared Reynolds, April Hamilton, Tom O'Connell, Doug Hembree, Chris Buice, Lester Lustbadder, Standing Tree Spirit Woman, Cosmo Holloway, Nex Grae, Rachel Whitlow, Andrea Henderson, Niles Haury, Hunter Bradshaw, Russ Bender, Zach Ross, Ryan Bradley, A. J. Kendall, Darren Langley, John Casteel, Warren Louis Pineda, Mike Jurca, Dale, Alex McKinnon, Johnny Sewell, Marla and "Jah-T" Allen, Alejandro, Ron Tate, Taylor Martin, Seth Oglesby, Justin and Whitney Talley, Nick Powell, Sarah Chambers, Matt and Ricky Lumpkin, The Harveys, The Coutants, Bob Petrella and Martin Zagaya, Keil and Lara Neff, Charles "Chuck" Cain, Tim Maholic, Meredith and Sara, Ryan Marrow, Topher, Chad Cornwell, Nathan Johnson, Leaf, Adam Bledsoe, Peggy Allman, Loretta, The Spears Family, especially Marley Jane, Lauren Clabourne, Nikki Henderson, Kelly Henderson, Amanda Owen, Vernon, Matt Marrow, Tonya Hope Lee Deckard, Freda and Shannon Wiggs, Troy Sass, Jim, Selena, and Anjelica, Kimberly Dowell, Cathy Poe, Peter Larry Daniel "George Costanza" Geros,

Brandon Atkins, Ashley Sunstrom, Tom Gaddis, Bill, Larry Dearing, Melvin Ellis, Mac, Aaron Brymer, Mathew Safadi, The Tharp Family, Rich Fredrick, Karen Kemmler, The Greenes, Jason Grahl, Jessica Conklin, Maney, T. J. Ensor, Lee Darden, Eric White, Jodi Vanderwoude, Kristi Wilcox, Launa, Robbie Overton, Benjaman Prijatel, Jonathan Roberts, Mason Booth, Marian, Stephen Loope, Pam Meadows, Anne Jackson, Heather Land, Tammy Dawn, Darrell Chandler, Terry Spratt, Leslie Anderson, Who Higgins III, Shaman, Roxanne, Scooter, Noel, Tex, Tommy, Rusty, Ginger, D. O. G., Tater Tot, Lon, Cornelius, Samantha, and Madeline.

This book would also not be possible if not for the comfort, guidance, and Enlightenment of Paramhansa Yogananda, Jesus Christ, Judas Thomas, St. Andrew, St. Bartholomew, St. James the Greater, St. James the Lessor, St. John, St. Jude, Judas Iscariot, St. Matthias, St. Matthew, St. Peter, St. Philip, St. Simon, Buddha, Maharaj, Khalil Gibran, C.S. Lewis, Neale Donald Walsh, Henry David Thoreau, Richard Bach, Joseph Campbell, Frank Oz, Shel Silverstein, Peter Sellers, Paul Neuman, Fred Rogers, Garrison Keilor, A. A. Milne, Jim Davis, Charles Shultz, Douglas Adams, St. Augustine, St. Valentine, Friedrich Wilhelm Nietzsche, Plato, Aristotle, Sir Isaac Newton, Carlos Castaneda , Jerzy Kosiński, Matthew Fox, Chuck Palaniuk, Dr. Seuss, The Tao Te Ching, Albert Einstein, Steven Hawkings, Steven King, Gustav Mahler, Wolfgang Amadeus Mozart, Joseph Shabalala, Sibongiseni Shabalala, Thamsanqa Shabalala,Thulani Shabalala, Msizi Shabalala, Albert Mazibuko, Abednego Mazibuko, Russel Mthembu, Muzi Sikhondze, Mfanufikile Zungu, Jockey Shabalala, Jabulani Dubazana, Inos Phungula, Ben Shabalala, Geophrey Mdletshe, Headman Shabalala, Milton Mazibuko, Funokwakhe Mazibuko, Joseph Mazibuko, Walter Malinga, Matovoti Msimanga, Frank Vincent Zappa, Ian Underwood, Joni Mitchell, Jimmy Carl Black, Roy Estrada, Davy Coronado,

Ray Hunt, Ray Collins, Robert Plant, Jimmy Page, John Paul Jones, John Bonham, Paul McCartney, John Lennon, George Harrison, Ringo Starr, Roger Daultery, Pete Townsend, John Entwhistle, Keith Moon, Trey Anastasio, Mike Gordon, John Fishman, Paige McConnell, Bob Segar, Willie Nelson, Al Jerreau, Billy Joel, Joel and Ethan Coen, Chuck Wein, Michael Chriton, Charlie Bacis, Bob Amacker, Phil Harris, Randy Newman, James Taylor, John Hughes, John Candy, Nicolaus Copernicus, Abraham Lincoln, Baron Bingen, Charlotte Blob, Jimmy Cameron, Thomas Jefferson, Hal Ashby, Gene Brewer, Mark Endes, Ed Cassidy, John Locke, Trent Reznor, Maynard James Keenan, Danny Carey, Justin Chancellor, Adam Jones, Bruce Lee, Jet Li, Bill Murray, Chevy Chase, Rodney Dangerfield, Mike Meyers, Dana Carvey, Kevin Smith, Jason Mewes, Jason Lee, Lawrence Kasdan, Chuck Jones, Johnny Hartman, Vladimir Vladimirovich Nabokov, Troy Duffy, Audrey Hepburn, Fred Astaire, Darrell Scott, Vince Guaraldi, Brad Nowell, Bud Gaugh, Eric Wilson, Zach del la Rocha, Tom Morello, Tim Commerford, Brian Wilson, Carl Wilson, Dennis Wilson, Billy Widner, Adam Sandler, Buck Henry, Mel Blanc, A. J. Russell, Richard Brautigan, J. D. Salinger, Kelsey Grammer, Jerry Seinfield, Larry David, Michael Richards, Jason Alexander, Ray Charles, Jim Varney, Jim Carey, Richard 'Pistol' Allen, Jack Ashford, Bob Babbitt, Benny 'Papa Zita' Benjamin, Eddie 'Bongo' Brown, Bootsy Collins, Johnny Griffin, Ben Harper, Joe Hunter, James Jameson, Uriel Jones, Montell Jordan, Gerald Levert, Joe Messina, Al Jardine, Kyle Cook, Bryan Yale, Paul Doucette, Adam Gaynor, Mike Love, Allison Krauss, Arlo Guthrie, Woody Guthrie, Eric Clapton, Peter Frampton, Marvin Gay, Carl Riener, Steve Vai, George and Ira Gerswin, Donald Fagen, Walter Becker, Denny Dias, Jeff "Skunk" Baxter, Jim Hodder, Billy Crystal, David Palmer, Oscar Wilde, Earnest Hemmingway, Robert Crumb, George Lucas, Mark Hamill, Harrison Ford, Carrie Fisher, James Earl Jones, Clint Eastwood,

Val Kilmer, Mark Twain, Stevie Ray Vaughn, Geddy Lee, Alex Lifeson, Neil Peart, David Allen Coe, Jack Johnson, John Coltrane, Rob Thomas, Garth Brooks, Bob Marley, Quentin Tarrantino, Roger Avery, Harry Neilson, David O. Selznick, Clark Gable, Vilian Ledigh, Leslie Howard, Olivia De Havilland, Werner Herzog, Timothy Treadway, John Houston, Martin Luther King, Jr., Frank J. Tippler, Edgar Allen Poe, Humphrey Bogart, Jimi Hendrix, Noel Redding, Mitch Mitchell, Robert Frost, Dylan Thomas, Tom Waits, Sting, Andy Summers, Stewart Copland, Ozzy Osbourne, Tony Lommi, Terence "Geezer" Butler, Billy Ward, James Hetfield, Lars Ulrich, Ron McGovney, Peter and Bobby Farrely, Dave Chappelle, Neal Brennan, Jim Breuer, Les Claypool, Johnny Cash, Al Green, Bella Fleck, Victor Wooten, Paul Simon, Dolly Parton, Lloyd Grant, Brad Parker, Jeff Warner, Yella Cameron, Barry De Predergast, Billy Cox, Hebie Fletcher, Paul Gebaur, Benny Harrison, Matt Stone, Trey Parker, Seth Macfarlane, Pat Hartley, Particia Higgens, Luke Hyneg, Michael Hynson, Barry Kanaiaupuni, Miss Mercy, Les Paul, Melinda Merryweather, David Nuuhiwa, Teresea Pinter, Allan Schuff, Steve Sutherland, Maureen Thorton, Donald Sutherland, Mark Whalberg, Leonardo Dicaprio, P. T. Anderson, Johnny Mathes, John C. Reilly, Richard Kelly, Randy California, Jay Ferguson. Christopher Guest, Meg Ryan, Rob Riener, Keifer Sutherland, Dustin Hoffman, Matt Groening, David X. Cohen, David Carradine, David Bowie, Richard M. Sherman, Robert B. Sherman, Anne Bancroft, Uma Thurman, Lilly Tomlin, Stanley Kubrick, Sean Penn, Alan Parker, Morgan Freeman, Jake Gyllenhaal, Hugh Prather, Stan Lee, Jerry Siegel, Joe Shuster, Arnold Schwarzenegger, Van Morrison, Tim Robbins, Martin Breast, Naomi Watts, Peter Jackson, Jack Bruce, Ginger Baker, Steven Tyler, Joe Perry, Tom Hamilton, Eddie and Alex Van Halen, David Lee Roth, Duane Allman, Butch Trucks, Dickey Betts, Berry Oakley, Jaimoe Johanson, Chris Squire, Steve Jobs, Jennifer

Connelly, Robert Rodriguez, Antonio Banderas, Alan White, Trevor Rabin, Tony Kaye, Greg Allman, Hank Williams, Sr., Bryan May, Roger Taylor, Freddie Mercury, John Decon, Kevin Bacon, Phillip Seymour Hoffman, Cathrine Ross, Robert Johnson, Robert Frost, Michael "Flea" Balzary, Beck Hansen, Michel Kang, Michael Travis, Bill Nershi, Kyle Moseley, Anthony Kiedas, Jack Irons, Hillel Slovak, B. B. King, Carlos Santana, Elvis Presley, Mathew Broderick, Terry Gilliam, Terry Jones, Graham Chapman, John Cleese, Eric Idle, Terry Jones, Michael Palin, Billy Corgan, James Iha, D'arcy Wrezky, Jimmy Chamberland, Perry Ferrell, Dave Navarro, Eric Avery, Steve Winwood, Jim Capaldi, John Medeski, Billy Martin, Oliver and Chris Wood, Mick Jagger, Kieth Richards, Ron Wood, Charlie Watts, Brian Jones, Mick Taylor, Ian Stewart, Jim Morrison, Ray Manzarek, John Densmore, Bon Scott, Brian Johnson, Angus Young, Malcolm Young, Cliff Williams, Phil Rudd, Dave Evans, Mark Evans, Chris Slade, Siman Right, Don Bluth, Stephen Perkins, Ravi Shankar, Norah Jones, Sarah McLachlan, Jewel, John Bell, John "JoJo" Hermann, Todd Nance, Domingo S. Orbitsz, Johnny Colt, Dave Schools, Cris Traynor, Gavin Rossdale, Jimmy Herring, Michael Houser, Nigel Pulsford, Dave Parsons, Robin Goodrige, Sacha Puttnan, Chris Robinson, Rich Robinson, Steve Gorman, Rob Colors, Sven Pipen, Paul Stacey, Eddie Harsch, Jeff Cease, Audely Freed, Greg Rzab, Andy Hess, Marc Ford, Bill Dobrow, Pauly Shore, Steven Baldwin, Vince Vaughn, Owen and Luke Wilson, Chris Cornell, Hirov Yamamoto, Klaus Voormann, Kim Thayil, Cheech Marin, Tommy Chong, Jerry Lewis, Dean Martin, Frank Sinatra, Jeff Amet, Stone Gossard, Mike McCready, Eddie Vedder, Matt Cameron, Travis Warren, Shannon Hoon, Christopher Thorn, Phil Spector, Roger Stevens, Brad Smith, Glen Graham, Tom and John Fogerty, Stu Cook, Doug Clifford, Syd Barrett, Bob Klose, Roger Waters, Richard Wright, Nick Mason, Levon Helm, Garth Hudson, Jim

Welder, Randy Ciarlante, Levon Helm, Jim Wieder, Mel Brooks, Randy Ciarlante, Richard Bell, Robbie Robertson, Rick Danko, Richard Manuel, Stan Szelest, Leon Russell, Roebuck 'Pops' Staples, Neil Diamond, Dr .John, Emmylou Harris, Bill Withers, Neil Young, Muddy Waters, Howlin' Wolf, Stevie Wonder, Elbridge "Al" Bryant, Melvin Franklin, Eddie Kendricks, Paul Williams, Dave Ruffin, Dennis Edwards, Richard Street, Damon Harris, Ron Tyson, Ali-Ollie Woodson, Theo Peoples, G. C. Cameron, Will Ferrell, Ray Charles, Louie Armstrong, Ella Fitzgerald, Betty Carter, Billie Holiday, Stan Getz, Miles Davis, Sammy Davis Jr., Prince, Alf, Dave Mathews, Dave Mustaine, David Wllefson, Greg Handevit, Jim Carrey, Adam Rifkin, Carl V. Dupre, Guiseppe Andrews, James Debello, Edward Furlong, Sam Huntington, Kate Winslet, Johnny Depp, Chris Farley, Gene Wilder, Ronald Dahl, Gilda Radner, Christopher Walken, Eric Stoltz, Tim Burton, Oliver Stone, Steve Martin, Keven Spacey, Chris Cooper, Paul Reubens, Michael Gondrey, Kurt Cobain, Dave Grohl, John Mayburry, Andy Griffith, Don Knotts, Ron Howard, Dorris Day, Steve Buscumi, Harold Ramis, Tom Blecker, Marc Rocco, Ivan Rietman, James Cameron, William Wisher, Jr., Ridley Scott, John Anderson, Brian O'Halloran, Jeff Ament, Matt Cameron, Mike D, Adrock, Iain Softley, Jeff Bridges, John Goodman, Phil Ehart, Billy Greer, Rich Williams, Steve Walsh, David Ragsdale, Mix Master Mike, Gene Kelly, Bing Crosby, Danny Kaye, Rosemary Clooney, George Clooney, Jude Law, Ewan McGreggor, Natalie Portman, Zach Braff, Danny Elfman, Danny Boyle, Irvine Welsh, Hayden Christensen, Alex Winter, Robert Zemeckis, Bob Gale, Christopher Lloyd, Michael J. Fox, Tom Warburton, Larne Michaels, Robert Stevenson, P. L. Travers, Bill Walsh, Hunter S. Thompson, Phillip K. Dick, William S. Burroughs, Richard Linklater, Roman Polanski, Darren Aronofsky, Sam Mendes, Woody Allen, Ken Kesey, Mario Puzo, Steven Spielberg, John Travolta, Francis Ford Coppola, Marlon

Brando, Al Pachino, James Caan, Samuel L. Jackson, Robert De Nero, Alec Guiness, Tim Roth, Bruce Willis, Rachel Weisz, Michael Madsen, Harvey Keitel, Tim Roth, Robert Duvall, Talia Shire, Diane Keaton, John Cazale, Richard S. Castellano, Abe Vigoda, Conan O'Brian, Andy Richter, Mel Gibson, Mario Puzo, Martin Scorsese, Cameron Crowe, Andy Kaufman, John Williams, Robin Williams, Charlie Kaufman, Nicolas Cage, John Malkovich, Benicio Del Toro, Alejandro González Iñárritu, Bill Hicks, Alex Jones, Mel Gibson, Robert Downey Jr., Hugh Jackman, Chris Smith, Ray Bradbury, Stuart Rosenberg, Andy and Larry Wachowski, Sergio Leone, David O. Russell, Mark Brochart, and Mike Shank.

Thank You All! God Bless You!!

In Loving Memory of

Bernice and Ronald Kunze

and

Arthur and Marie Pugh

Who Planted the Seed of a Perfect Love

TABLE OF CONTENTS

Dedications — v

Introduction: The Fruit is Calling From the Trees — xvii

A Letter from the Author — xxi

Preface — xxv

BOOK ONE
Staring into the Sun: The Death of Lucifer — 1

BOOK TWO
Death of Colors: A parable — 15

BOOK THREE
Becoming Peace: A Guidebook — 41

INTRODUCTION:

The Fruit is Calling From the Trees

"The fruit is calling from the trees," means to beware of the meaningless Thoughts and Knowledge that is all around you.

> Uncontrolled Thoughts are what, since the beginning of Enlightenment, have been referred to as demons. Over-translation has robbed them of meaning, making them imagery instead of allegorical. Please be careful of your Thoughts, Mind, and Ego. The difference between Knowledge and Wisdom is that Wisdom is the overwhelming presence of FEELING and Knowledge simultaneously. If FEELING is not present, it's just another product of Ego, just meaningless words, and just another book on a shelf.

Suffering is the greatest lesson we all will ever learn. As soon as it's accepted as part of this Life, the acceptance of suffering is the beginning of Enlightenment. Denial of suffering leads to uncontrolled Thoughts, demons, taking control of your mind. The completely uncontrolled Mind is insanity (the devil), but is helpless against the presence of Hope, the subconscious belief in the Truth, in Love, and that all of Life's moments have Meaning. This belief is subtle, but feeling has kept calling us to it through Feeling not Thought, but we keep falling to our Minds, to rationality and denial, because we are human. Enlightenment is the moment you don't let your Mind win anymore. Enlightenment is being so full of Hope and Peace that you stop thinking completely, living completely in Meditation.

Meditation Is the Art of God Awareness.

Love will always be stronger than confusion, because with Love, you realize confusion is meaningless. It is your Ego that keeps pulling mankind down the rabbit hole of meaningless Knowledge in pursuit of the Truth and the Meaning of Life.

The Meaning of Life is Feeling and is beyond words, beyond concepts, and beyond Thoughts. Only through not thinking will you *feel* the very thing you've always been seeking.

There is no greater Hell than Intelligent Confusion.

Only Love will reigns over Hell, demons, and the devil. See the Truth beneath the surface of things. Be in complete control of every Thought through Mastering the Art of not thinking and through Complete Awareness of Feeling.

When you only do what *feels* right, you will receive everything you will ever want and become wiser then all Minds, but need not to prove anything to anyone, nor hide from anything.

You will feel the Passion in every Soul. It is a True Angel that has the ability to see the Soul through every Mind. All Souls are One, divided by Mind.

Daniel Arthur Zagaya 6/18/06

True Reflection goes Beyond one's own image.

A Letter from the Author:

Dear Reader,

You are one of the few Souls who might most understand the Greatest Secret I've ever kept.

Please listen closely and carefully to this letter. God has brought me to you and you to me for a reason no matter how "small." You are enlightened and talented and can help me bring Peace internationally.

This is the tip of the iceberg.

When I was a child, I was unique in the loosest term the word can be used. My relationship with God I kept very personal, simply because I was afraid if I tried to explain it, everyone would be convinced I was insane.

God has spoken to me directly my entire Life. God not only communicated with me through the Voice of Voices, amplified Infinitely outward from the innermost core of my Being, louder than everything and anything else, but also exoterically in the outward projection of my Universe through Everyone and Everything.

But, the older I got, I started to realize this relationship, this Reality, was uncommon. My Mind became divided, and the Truth was no longer Whole, but in two co-existent paradoxical Truths which I later found out were only sides of the Ultimate Truth. But, as you know, division can be contagious.

The Spirit that was (and Is) God seemed to begin to leave me as I began to doubt my Self. I started to mistake The Truth with the opposite of the Truth. I began to need outside approval to fill the void I blamed God for leaving.

Need for outside approval caused me to doubt and fear myself and God. As you know, through fearing and doubting part of my Self and God, I feared and doubted all of my Self and God.

This paradoxically caused me to create the opposite of everything I wanted to have, feel, and be.

This process continued until I was 15, and I was trapped in a false universe in fear of a non-existent angry god my Mind made real. My Mind has always had the power to do this; except now, it was working against me. I was controlled by my greed and owned by my fear, trapped in a false dimension of cold emptiness.

I was a prisoner of this false universe that was controlled by a side of myself I considered, at the time, to be not of God, and was the victim of ownership by the concept of a demi-god who would control me with fear and greed that paralyzed me.

This demi-god within me become so powerful it began to "wear" me, and I was convinced I was helpless, hopeless. This demi-god came from the "side" of me that is (and was) the deepest, darkest, coldest, farthest side of me and God. (Which are all adjectives for the lowest frequency.)

This demi-god (Which is the same as the Alter-Ego or What I Am Not) had the audacity to try to convince me that not only was he not part of God, but also out of God's control, therefore more powerful than God.

At my lowest, weakest point, God, the Voice of Voices, finally reappeared to dominate my dark side with the Highest Logic and irrefutable counter-points.

This Voice assured me that there is nothing that isn't God, even the opposite of God, and even the opposite of God is still God, just in the lowest form. God taught me that God, and only God, had the ability of being the opposite of God, and that the Truly Most Powerful Master is *Co*-Master and *Co*-Creator with God because God is Everything. I just needed to trust God, and the time will come. The Time is Now. Fear and greed will never own me again. I know now proportion is relative to perspective. Anything divided from God can only logically be half as powerful then its Source (God) and itself at all times, division being the seed of its own destruction. Unity with God *is Power.*

The upward climb of the illusion of time is becoming more and more evident.

God asked me then to write books to serve as a parable and a guidebook to the New Spirituality. God told me he would tell me the second book at 15, entitled, 'Death of Colors'. The third, he would tell me at age 20, entitled 'Becoming Peace.' And I didn't find out about Book 1 until I was 21.

Thank you for what you have done for me and the world.

I have never have trusted anyone with these books until I had certainty of their Source.

I'm certain.

These books are what I am doing and what I have learned.

No one else understands like you do. I know. You know. God knows.

Peace Be With You,

Daniel Zagaya

Preface

Isn't It amazing how paradoxical Life Is? I embrace every element of Everything. I pulled myself to the darkest corners of the Universe to prove to my Self for certain that there isn't anything that God isn't, and I have. The Ego tries to tell us and everyone otherwise. Pride is false power, an apathetic prison of greed controlled by fear.

I've realized that God already Speaks to me through Everything. When Thought speed is completely slowed down, you are literally able to break off all the adverbs, adjectives, and all other gratuitous definitions; You Hear the Highest Form of Your Self, which Is the Voice of God.

The interesting thing about Knowing what the Highest Form of Your Self Is, to define it, you must know what the opposite, or the lowest form, of your Self is. You can't define the Self any other way than paradoxically defining the Id, the Ego, or simply Who We Aren't. Be completely aware of Who You Aren't without question, and you paradoxically define your Self, undivided. When one must live with the opposite of themselves to consistently know themselves paradoxically, as all do, you might as well Master it, become best friends with it through a dark period to Knowing for certain, exactly who you aren't, and to recognize the voice that isn't you. I know this sounds crazy, and to many standards it is. But, who is anybody to say what crazy is? God was and Is my psychiatrist, literally.

I began to recognize God was communicating with me when I was 15; The Voice of Truth began to tell me the Secrets of the Universe. Eventually, there is a brutal Conscious struggle between defining the Self and Ego, dividing them with awareness of empathetic association or emotional core in association with each existing Thought, so they can paradoxically define each other.

When the Self and "Anti-Self" are established to the Perspective that you are, a new neuron net is formed when your brain simultaneously recognizes paradoxical Truth and direct Truth simultaneously. That is when you begin to realize God is literally constantly communicating to, through, and with You and Everything. This is the Process of God Consciousness.

As You Know, Everything Is Pure Energy. God in God's Highest Form Is the Ultimate Father Managing All Energy and dimensions and Is Pure Love and Pure Beauty, and indefinably, simply Is.

You have been chosen to define your Journey for You and Everyone.

Thank You for Listening.

BOOK ONE

STARING INTO THE SUN:
The Death of Lucifer

The moments when Jesus was arguing with Lucifer were the moments of Consciousness where His Soul and Id were combating as The Source of Truth.

Obviously, God is the Source of Truth, but is also the Source of Everything, the Source of Sources. Now, as the Masters of Our Time have already shared with you, God can only be at the Highest Form with a lower form to choose from. God, to experience the God Self, had to divide the God Self and create a paradox or opposite of the God Self. Everything can only be defined from the perspective of what it isn't.

The Likeness of the Personality of God was expressed to and through Jesus through the Archangel Michael. Michael spoke to and Through Jesus, just as Jesus speaks to and Through Us. But, the Voice of Christ can only be defined through co-existence of the voice of the opposite of the Likeness of God's Personality, Michael, and that co-existent voice is the voice of Lucifer.

Lucifer is the opposite of the Truth, which exists consciously, so the Truth can be the Truth. Lucifer is part of God and You, the lowest part, present to define the Highest paradoxically.

When Jesus was arguing with Lucifer, in a way he was arguing with part of God and part of Himself in the Process of defining what God is through what God isn't.

When Jesus realized Lucifer was just Paradoxical Truth, God began talking to Him directly *and* paradoxically bringing Lucifer completely in the 5th charka, making Him Completely Christ in the 7th charka.

I would like to make a clarifying addition to my last point. I don't want anyone to think there is any power equal to God, God is Power; God Is Everything. By that definition, there is no Devil, or opposite power equal to God, but there are devils that are simply low level Angels controlled by their fears, greed, pride, and apathy through the communication of false evidence and illusions of separation created by Lucifer, the lord of devils.

Lucifer is the perspective that is the cosmic definition of the illusion of the separation from God, and in complete denial of his complete attachment to God defines himself as the paradox of God, the master of fear, and The Angel of Death.

Lucifer is God's spiteful, rebellious servant.

In a way Lucifer is a prisoner of his own definitions and his own delusions. The Lucifer perspective was a necessity to Destiny to create something to "graduate" to the Metaphysical World from, and to create a perspective to see God from to be able to use free will to "Become God".

Without Lucifer's existence, there would be no Process. The Process is to Evolve in Awareness from the physical world to the Metaphysical world through the Imagination and Esoteric Awareness. True Masters are impervious to Lucifer's power because of Awareness of True Power, God Unity.

A Master can see God in the opposite of God even when the opposite of God can not see God in himself/herself, guiding the opposite of God to the Self, Christ.

When Christ said, "Don't let your left hand know what the Right Hand is doing..." the Right Hand is the Christ or

The Truth

Self, and the left hand is the Id, Lucifer, or the opposite of the Self.

Lucifer used to be the Right Hand of The Father until becoming so drunk with envy to want to be the one and only True God; it caused him to divide himself from his Self. This, by default, created the self-definition of the opposite of God.

Lucifer is God's Prodigal Son. God loves him as equally as his other Sons (and Daughters, though Sons is commonly from Heirs, and was never intended to be limited to male). God is Love Completely. Through Lucifer's Self-division he can never have more than half of even his own Power. But, the moment he becomes completely Conscious of God's Unconditional Love, the physical world will complete itself, and completely evolve into the Metaphysical, undivided.

The Prophecy will be fulfilled when Lucifer forgives God, forgives himself, and makes Peace with God, Everything, and Everyone. God always Loves and Forgives Lucifer; God is Love and Forgiveness. Their Peace will be completely made.

It is impossible for this not to happen; it is Destiny. The moment Lucifer, God's prodigal Son, realizes the only Power is through God, and that he is an extension of God and Everything, is the moment the Kingdom of God will return.

Something I feel necessary to clarify is what looks like a small typographical error.

When I said, "Lucifer used to be the Right Hand of the Father until becoming so drunk with envy to want to be the True God, it caused him to divide himself from his Self. This, by default, created the self-definition of the opposite of God…"

I want to make it completely clear it was Lucifer that became drunk with envy, not God, but the confusing part of this is that Lucifer was (and is) still part of God.

So in theory it was God, as a "less magnificent" part of Himself, becoming drunk with envy at the Magnificent part of Himself, using the gift of free will he gave that part of himself against and Himself, creating the birth of dichotomy, and the less magnificent "separated" form of himself as a logical necessity.

In a way, it wasn't even Lucifer's fault; it was (and Is) God's Will. This conflict of logic between God and one of His Sons was inevitable to define the True God and the Kingdom of God.

In theory, Lucifer thought, "If I am part of God, and there isn't anything God isn't, and reality is a manifestation of my free will, how am I not God, and aren't I the one that holds the True Power?"

In a way, he was Right and wrong at the same time.

He lacked the Imagination and Power to realize he was "inside" God and that God was "inside" Him. He was "cut from the cloth," not The Cloth Itself. His lack of Conscious Unity with God caused the absence of Spirit.

His pride and greed blinded him from being able to see beyond himself or connect himself with Everything. These "dark" questions caused him to divide from God consciously with free will and blind himself in frustration from the ability to Love. Darkness is simply the absence of Light. These questions tortured him with a never-ending greed for complete Glory.

Everything is Reflection of Light.

Lucifer couldn't accept sharing the Power with God, and his greed and the Energy It created transformed him.

But, this was part of God's Process.

Before God gave birth to Self-division through Lucifer, the Kingdom of God wasn't Glory, something to be earned, or "worthy of," it just was, and was all there was. It had nothing to be compared to, therefore, nothing to earn; it was all that existed.

There's no reason Lucifer wouldn't have a God complex, and that's what God wanted and needed to paradoxically define Truth.

Without Lucifer, God isn't Magnificent, He just Is.

But, thanks to Lucifer's choice to deny his Creator, we know what magnificence is through what it isn't. We can have darkness as a counter-perspective of something to grow from.

It was Lucifer's destiny to define the "isn't" and be the "isn't." When mankind collectively realize the "isn't" is part and the same as the "Is" paradoxically through the illusions of Lucifer, he will complete his definition, and share True Power at God's Mercy, becoming One with God once again and return to the Kingdom of to God for Eternity.

Now once Our Minds can hear God both directly *and* paradoxically, You and I are United with the Source.

The Source, All That Is, Is simply Invisible Self-existent Substance bound and formed into "matter" through consciousness, or through the self-applied "definitions" we choose to see or create to "personalize" our Universal Awareness of an indefinable Reality.

Eventually, our definitions become us, as we become our definitions.

We are born to fall in Love with Creation Itself. Definition itself is a form of Creation, as well as mankind's inescapable addiction.

The addiction of definition becomes a language unto itself that becomes so personal you are trapped as a prisoner or the bounds of your own words, your own definitions.

You forget you're hearing a language you taught yourself it speaks so quickly now…

Quickly compared to what?

You can't be the voice if you hear it, it is a *part* of you, just as *everything* is a part of you, and you are part of God and Everything.

Language itself takes its own voice within you, using the Mind to be a step ahead of the brain.

All voices within you, spoken or unspoken, are *parts* of you.

You are not them, they help to define your Self.

Language seems to be The Answer instead of the question.

Language is simply the self-defined expression that allows us to perceive inwardly to The Answer that is beyond language.

All expression is both the beginning and end of Creation. Consciousness becomes real Through Spirit. We create bounds with the definitions we choose to let limit us.

All of Existence is Consciousness and Spirit.

Consciousness continuously divides Itself with and into "smaller" and "smaller" words, voices, images, sides, symbols, and perspectives, until the smallest part is connected with The Largest.

Consciousness Is an Ever-growing World Within Itself.

Mastery is to Know, share, and understand all definitions of the indefinable, not just as your own, but accepting them as paradoxically subjective definitions of concepts without bounds.

Do we give Power to words, or do they give Power to themselves?

Though, the gathering of definitions is gathering of information, and gathered information is gathered Power. Knowledge and Power are Self-defined, the same *and* different.

Though, wouldn't the Highest Master be the Master of the language that created the definitions, as opposed to a collection of the definitions themselves?

What defines the language, and what is the source of these definitions? Wouldn't mastery of language be known through mastering the language we use to communicate with Our Self? Is the language we use to communicate to Our Self the same as the one God uses to communicate to us with?

What is the Self?

What is God?

What isn't?

Who am I to ask these questions?

Who am I to answer them?

Who am I not?

Do we decide the definitions of these questions, or do they define us? Is there a wrong answer to these questions?

Who am I to say what wrong is?

These definitions I am deciding this moment aren't deciding my Life; they *are* my Life.

I define and am defined by what I choose to see at every moment…

There are those in this world who feel that they see

what they don't want to see…

Is it that they can't choose what they define as their wants, or that they can't choose what they see? What or who chooses what they see, what everyone sees? Is it a language or voice of undesired possibilities or even realities infecting their Imagination?

Does everyone need this?

Does knowing why end the need and reality of its presence?

All psychological need for definition will exist because it is how Our Reality is created and mastered.

Creation and Mastery are why we're here.

You free yourself from any obsession by understanding, yet detaching, yourself from any voice within you that wants and needs, using every other side and voice within you to understand why that one voice is not complete, and would "want" or "need."

Everything is only the definition we apply.

Music wouldn't be music if not for the knowledge of the notes you don't want to play. Just the same, you wouldn't be if not for the knowledge of the words you don't want to say.

Mastery of language is not only Mastery of Self, but also Mastery *of* Itself.

In a way, darkness, pain, and suffering are probably some of Life's greatest lessons. Beyond redefining personal ability, there are monumental revelations coming from these experiences.

The first is that the consumption of much of the suffering in this world is the result of the Mind's conscious or subconscious obsession with the feeling that is the result of suffering.

This feeling is the result of sensory overload of powerful elements and conditions that surround us on this Earth.

When the Mind obsesses on these things or on the feeling that comes from these things, or even the mental exhaustion that comes from obsession itself, a subconscious obsession transforms our time on this Earth from a conscious dream to a conscious nightmare.

The second lesson that is learned from suffering comes from the analysis of pain. Beyond leaning how to avoid unnecessary inflictions comes a deeper lesson… Acceptance.

With The Perspective of Acceptance, a Being retrospectively sees the many vices and forms of denial he or she has used to avoid these overwhelming, but temporary incontinences of pain.

The Id or Ego tries to convince us that your suffering is greater than your Universal Brothers and Sisters.

It is what it is.

All suffering is relative to subjectivity, equalizing through empathy.

Through Christ, God has taught us to make Our Souls strong enough to control the devil in Our Minds through teaching conscious separation between the Soul and Mind, so the Soul can reconnect to being a part of Everything.

The Truth

Christ shared the God Perspective. Within it, he could see Lucifer, the opposite of God, inside the minds of man, government, and religion. He saw the conscious divisions mankind were making with through the Lucifer perspective owning them through ignorance and fear.

He knew something must be done to return the attention of mankind's perspective toward God, and because God was His Greatest Love, His will was God's Will.

Christ knew of Lucifer's possession over the Collective Consciousness was the seed of self-destruction, hypnotizing them with fear, hate, pride, and greed.

He knew if he told mankind that Lucifer was only in and controlled them through their Minds, they would never listen. So, He and his closest Brothers recorded such a profound collection of self-evident Truth, His Will would inevitably be done. But, the actions of His Life had to be in harmony to his Divine Logic. He would have to irrefutably prove God's Unconditional Love and Mercy and his Divine Compassion for all mankind. His Conscious Will of sacrificing Himself to and with God was the image He and God decided on.

Though, Collective Consciousness was not an immediate return, but the beginning of the Process of Complete Collective Enlightenment.

When Christ sacrificed Himself to God, He returned to the Ultimate Father in Heaven and United in One Body with His and Everyone's Highest Form, the Angel of Peace, to return to the Earth in the Form of Spirit.

The Spirit of Christ lives and speaks *to* and *through* You and Everyone. Often, many are still limited by hearing words that are not Christ.

By Awareness of Spirit, or the Feeling at the core of your Being, You can recognize the Voice that Is and the voice isn't Christ. The words you say or hear without feeling are simply either unconscious or the opposite of Christ, which, through Awareness, paradoxically turns your perspective towards the Inner-Christ.

In the process of denying Energy to every voice within your mind that isn't Christ, eventually your brain will create a new pattern where Christ is the only Voice You Hear. This Process Is God Consciousness. The moment you consciously achieve The Process of God Consciousness, your body Is a Portal of the Spirit, and You Are The Light.

It is every human's Destiny to return to God Completely, Through The Christ That Is already speaking to You through your Mind and Everything.

> For All of You Who Already Know All of This,
> "Welcome back to Heaven."

BOOK TWO

DEATH OF COLORS:
A parable

The Truth

Tex's eyes were glazed with the blinding dust of despair. He could still smell his Brother's life hovering like a cloud in the dry choking dust. The stirring air was glowing with sunlight. Tex tried thinking back to before it all evaporated into disaster.

His Brother's empty eyes still smiled. Tex's turned stomach ached with the timeless downward spiral of nauseating confusion and regret. He stared at his Brother's dead eyes, and his blood seeping into the Texas ground.

Tex picked up his Brother's bleeding corpse and threw it upon the back of his horse. Tears were rolling down his face by now. He wiped the blood from his hands and climbed upon his saddle. The entire town exhaled in silent relief. Tex remained silent.

The sun seemed to get closer and closer.

The Texas sky will always remind him of his Brother's blood. He had to get out of this place. He could no longer tell blood from tears as despair hit his tongue.

An Indian sits by a fire with tears running down His face. At first glance, He seemed to be a warrior, but by the look of His Eyes, no blood had ever been shed by Those Hands.

"Their faces seemed to resemble glass," He said to no one. He felt compulsions of joy, yet His Face remained still.

He saw Their Souls. He saw the decades of breaths shared by the lungs of birds slightly gliding, waiting for Life to begin again.

"You can not read eyes," He screamed. His melted with tears, but They were Tears of Joy as smiles taunted Him through glass faces.

Freedom meant nothing, for It was all He knew. The aches of despair possessed by men of 'civil' surroundings were less meaningful than the gray ash speaking of its own silent envy of Flame.

THE Trees danced as the Music of the katydids poured through the leaves. They were laughing, laughing at the lost strangers wandering in life to find it all behind them.

Only when you speak to This Symphony of Trees, will you breathe in the Wisdom exhaled by Prophets.

The Cracklings of Flames are Poems of Nature, and only when you inhale Its Spirit, will you consume Its Wisdom.

The moon spoke of nearly midnight.

Tex rode to the tiring limit of his aspirations. The calling of evaporating Wisdom bleaching the sky pulled him to the flames of redemption.

Tex was tired and weary.

He saw the Indian was dancing with His feet digging into the embers. And, the TRUTH of agony subtly scorns His feet as He is harmoniously chanting,

"Crying in his actions, the dust still stirs.
Upon the spilt blood of his kin,
The River slowly flows.
And, upon it you shall know:

The Truth

The TRUTH of Spirit,
The doorways of Wisdom
Beyond your own world,
To a world where colors come to die,
Upon Rainbow Brook."

The Indian gazed at him with misunderstanding sympathy.

"Your face too is glass"

JUST take a moment to alter Perspective.

Feel the questions that need no Answer. Into confusion we fall first hand, into the Mind of another.

Deep into his mind he fell. Fall with him we shall, into the bottom of his burning eyes, into the bottom of his Imagination.

(See Reality through the Perspective of Tex's eyes.)

The Indian slowly handed me a long pipe about the size of His Arm. It is wrapped with Colorful ribbons, and looking to be made of wood and bone.

The generosity in His Eyes relieved me of any hesitation. I accepted with a subtle expression of appreciation. Though I had quit smoking as a young man, I considered it as a cool blanket to temporarily aid my troubled path.

I remember the Indian focusing into my wandering eyes. His Eyes were like Endless Tunnels watching as I fell into an Endless Pit of Color. A swirling Calm grasped my Pulse.

I remember His Voice slowly fading into a crescendo with the ease of a Sunset.

His Voice didn't come to my ears, but beyond them. And, like tapping Waves of Energy, it captured my Mind and altered my perception.

"Don't be alarmed, for the smoke of Wisdom will comfort you. Fall into The Stream for which is your Echoing Energy, and Flow.

Relax; floating down The Stream may be a heavy weight upon your Sanity, but think of it as AN ABSORBANT RIVER OF VELVET TIME. You gather confusion, thinking and forgetting, letting Thoughts and worries fall upon you, passing through you in swarming panic. Panic will only choke your will to swim.

He who flutters will be consumed.

And, lost you will be with your with your rapid beating Heart, consumed into the Castles of Ocean. If it senses your fear it will put you down with every struggle.

And, as you stair from the bottom of a worthless drowning Mind, choking from anxiety, you will fall.

You will fall deeper into the end and dead to the willing. And, with your last gasp of sight, you are but to see a man relaxing upon that same River.

The man floating would have realized to enjoy and survive the experience, he will need to relax and enjoy the ride, and flow with the MUSIC OF THE RIVER.

UNDERSTAND by not UNDERSTANDING, and not wanting to UNDERSTAND.

> Free your fears,
> Let it do unto you
> And take you away.
> Don't try to figure it out.
> See it as it all goes by."

TEX'S MIND WAS IN FULL CRECENDO NOW.

Two rabbits stopped him, Red with fur, to ask him what happiness was. "To see your Mind's potential whispered Vision of Pleasure," I replied.

I met a Tree as I was floating down The River. He told me,
> "Do not worry of the effects of worry,
> see the potential of Hope."

I saw myself in Their Eyes to realize what I was missing in my eyes.

Bleeding foxes smiled as I went by on The River. They were crying a white noise followed with abrupt mechanical cries.

The Tree also said,
"Do not look at the footprints behind ME, but where you are going.

THE SUN WILL ALWAYS BE YOUR BEST FRIEND.

Once I was worried what it was like to be worried, to gaze on a throbbing mind of worry. I worried that worry would become my fate. Worry won't ever make a man gaze willingly into Life, but will drive him closer to DEATH."

The Tree smiled, but its face remained still.

It simply smiled with its EYES.

My throat began to feel of stone lava.

I started to discover the voices inside me.

Dragons danced in my stomach barricaded by the stone lava.

The River surrounded my body. I tried to remember what the Indian had told me.

STILL DOWN THE RIVER I DRIFT.

I have never noticed The Colors in the sky before. NEVER HAVE I REALIZED THE MANY DIFFERENT SHADES OF **BLACK**.

The Stars gazed upon me, surrounding me, confounding me. They told me things. They told me of the Meaning of Twilight as their smiles helped to ease my rapid breaths.

I woke up with a layer of dew glistening from the already awakened dawn.

I felt as if it were the first time I had wakened in years.

I had blisters on my hands smothered in Black ash. I WAS ALONE. The Indian had left me and took His Wisdom With Him.

I was not where I had last been. The Trees were all gone and the air was dry.

I was now in a desert with a glistening Brook to my side. It mesmerized me. It radiated with the Colors of a pastel sky raining in its REFLECTION.

I gazed alone at the pastel skies, a baby cries, but my eyes see no one.

I'M LOST. I see Silver Mountains far in the distance. The Sun bled off my silver mountains, off its rocks made of mirrors.

I looked into the Colorful Brook flowing deeper and deeper into the pastel sand. A Fish came up to the surface, its scales with Colors gliding, dancing; caressing its dark shades of BLACK.

The Colors were moving, glowing, and The Fish seemed to be wallowing in melancholy. I believe he was unaware of his gliding Colors on black skin.

The Fish came up to me with tears in his eyes and said,

"The world had never been so cruel. The Waters in This Brook are shimmering with Clarity. Its Purity is such an essence that Colors come here to die. The Stars are jealous from miles away that We are able to share something so Beautiful."

"Then why are You sad," I said with devoted concern.

"It is the only one left! I have squirmed through burning waters. I have soaked so many poisons through My scales my Beautiful glimmer has turned to **Black**.

My soul is tortured, crippled! My blood is rotten! My Mind aches! Many years I have come looking for Rainbow Brook. I have come here to die, but Death is an underrated gateway; it is a contemplated exit, a rationalization. Only then does Rainbow Brook exist."

I objected with great haste.

"Have I died? My skin still breathes of Pink youth. If you could see The Beauty, the Rainbows dancing without dimension upon dark shadow night scales!"

"Beauty is only on the inside, and my inside is of a sick stone. Pain oozes through me slowly, anticipating my slow departure, driving me to the end of Rainbow Brook.

I saw you here the other day. Your hair was shorter than, and you had more panic in your eyes, but it was you.

You are lucky.

Many do not make it from the frenzied grasp of panic's twisting fate hurling them to the bottom.

But, you survived. Who showed you? It was the Creator of Colors wasn't it?"

"Who?"

"The Creator of Colors, the Indian."

"Oh, yes, what is His name?"

"He has no name, He has no need for it. He is the Creator; He has created All you see.

He brought the Rainbows; He gave them a pleasant place to die. He created this place, This Brook, as a Shrine of Beauty for Beauty. It is where Beauty comes to die.

He has used all He could to create this Endless MURAL OF RESPECT."

I inhaled tickling phlegm streaming down my snout, for a second I thought it was blood.

I started to dance to the music of the sky. It seemed to have the metallic vibrations of mosquito wings. I began to grow a little tired, but I tried fighting it.

I did not want to miss one second of This Intense Beauty gifted to me through the Red Skies of The Impossible.

My eyes got heavier with a breath of gravity deteriorating my strength.

I FELT LIKE WATER.

I knew what was happening through this experience of my most abstract figments of my sensuality, I faded.

I sank deeper until darkness was all I breathed.

Wandering down the trail, I sighed. The Trees smelled of Nature, and the dirt rose from the destruction of my travel.

I arose again to find days of beard expanding from my face. Hair was now flowing freely in long curls, gently wandering in the delicate wind.

A mist flew from my breath as if in an Antarctic November, spreading into a vapor, scattering into the empty sky.

I looked around in confusion. Where am I? The air grew warm against my cheeks, though the mist still steamed from my breath.

All The Seasons Were At Once. The leaves turned to fall in auburn colors of Death. Icicles hung from the branches, yet a heat rose to the glazing boarders of Summer.

Spreading across the radiant Colors of Ocean flow Colors above me.

I walked for miles. I never slept. My eyes seemed to be lost in time. I felt as if I could walk for years, never to feel tired, I walked for years.

Sorrow's gaze blinded by resting Souls lost me a long time ago. I had been lost inside the horizon to never find an End or a Beginning.

I was lost, and never want to be found.
Never could I feel the effects of Forever.

Years had passed that my eyes remained open.
I walked _over_ time.

I tread over sand of every Color, with its texture of flower, and the calm of White November Snow.

There were Two Suns.
One was always setting, and one was always rising.

Never was there reached a noon.

> Never did it reach the peak of rise
> unto the bright, Colorful sky.

> It always was the dusk's glow colliding
> with the Colors of dawn,
> the comfort of rest,
> and the calmness of DEATH.

Once I came to a field. It was Golden with the Flames of a Wild Breath of Life.

Flowers, Everywhere. Some towered high above my head. They had the golden shine of Sun glowing ocean, calmly breathing.

Alive was the soil, giving Life to every Color, lack of Life catching up, creating a confusing nausea upon Perception.

Hoofbeats.

Hoofbeats coiled air's Reflection upon Gold Oceans. Oh, it hurt, Silence broken after Eternity with shattering infliction.

Pain and relief melted into worry.

Hoof beats?

The air vibrated with the percussion of fear.

Standing in the distance upon Golden Sand stood a man upon a horse.

The man's flesh was Red, not unlike the embers that brought me to this state of Mind.

The horse approached me, and in its mouth laid a diamond.

And, as I peered into the diamond, the horse said to me, speaking with great prophesies.

And, into my quivering face, he said,

"Crying in his actions, the dust still stirs.
Upon the spilt blood of his kin,
The River slowly flows.
And, upon it you shall know:
The TRUTH of Spirit,
The doorways of Wisdom
Beyond your own world,
To a world where colors come to die,
Upon Rainbow Brook.

You have been lost in the time of wrong. I only speak in great concern, for you have been mourned upon many, and they speak in the same concern as I demonstrate,

'We will miss his vigilantly impair. To save us from the path of wrong was turned, but we wish it to return. The town is in ruins upon the same fate causing you to leave.'

In anger, regret, and revenge, an entire town yearns to see the man they thought was on their side."

I remained in confusion to recall the town that despised my approach. No enemies I thought to have disclosed without diminishment.

The Love for my own Brother had been overpowered by evil. Never I hope to return.

The Truth

Betrayal is a hideous Color.

The Power to Remember is but in New Eyes, and to See is to Remember, but to Remember is a poor excuse of the Mind.

Memory can alter by drugs, Dream, and discovery, and a Truth created unnaturally can be thrown together in a war to See and a war to Know, compelling and competing with each other for Happiness.

I have seen The Red Skies, but I have reached them naturally – as I hoped.

But, I know this is not the Truth.

The Truth can be confusing,

And, the fight to discover can be painful.

But, somewhere there is a man that can reach These Skies at will.

I am not him.

He can reach These Skies without substance, and this is The One that I seek.

Now has reached the magical hour.

Ahead, upon The Greatest of Hills will become of my future.

I felt a Calm I haven't reached for ages. I again found The Brook, and began to follow it.

I aspired to climb beyond the Silver Mountains, bleeding with Color.

My desire was to find The Creator, the Mind and the Soul that could create such beautiful scenes.

Approaching, I considered The Beauty of Odd and how the Music of Change is the Knowledge of What's Original.

The Brook became consumed into a wall of glistening rock.

Here was to be found The Tallest Mountain of Green, Blue, and Gray. Reflections beamed off its surface, surrounding me.

I could not turn back. It seemed back did not exist ~
                                            only Beyond.

Lost, I remained, in the Ocean of Paradise, and the next step to my trek was found above This Sheet of Colorful Stone.

I seeped my hands into The Wall, and my fingers dug into it like clay.

I had no fear of falling, for nowhere else could I fall to end this conception of what seemed to be Beyond what fatality brings.

Further I climbed to find Life and Beauty flourish as my altitude increased.

The higher I approached grew more LIFE.

Trees extended perpendicularly balanced, and I too was altered in this vertical balance of gravity.

I could walk again amidst the glorious Trees, glistening with Silence, with ease to find I was nearly to the top.

It turned to springtime within the magical hour.

At the edge, I was greeted by the humanity of a young boy.

He seemed almost Illuminated, his flesh blanketed with radiant Red.

"You have made it. You were desperately awaited, but you have arrived at a time without Hope.

Your aid of Mind will be appreciated upon the aftermath of the War of the Red feathers. Come."

I followed the boy to the top of the ridge to see many Towns of colors.

Underneath me, I could see Cities entirely blanketed in a Single Hue. I began to cry upon seeing These Glorious Towns of Vibrant Hue.

Far in the distance I saw Angelic Clouds of Sanity, like evaporating fantasy.

Each town was divided by Color. At the border of each City lay another differing with entirely different Color, attitudes, and moods.

All would change, but all remain pleasant in their own way.

To the bottom of The Silver Mountains spreading to the distant horizon, I could see the City of White.

The Trees were mesmerizing with their branches of ivory delicately dangling like glass snowflakes.

On the ground and spreading through the breeze were Heavenly Clouds of Shimmering Snow.

Every delicate grain of sand and glittering rock radiated with White.

Touching each individual city remained the flowing Rainbow Brook,

>inhaling beauty's Death,

>>Radiating LIFE.

Every town touched The Brook, not One Color remained untouched.

>Each color seeped into The Brook.
>Each and every Color of every Town,
>and Towns of every Color flowed into The Brook.

Immediately, I became very tired and hungry as humanity caught up with me.

I remained astonished as my Mind began to move faster than my body, and I grew faint.

The Truth

I shall fade upon this roadside in slumber.

I awoke to see the Creator looking back at me. I felt the impulse to jump up in surprise, but my body was too weak.

"Come with Me, My Son," and away We went.

"Where are We going?"

"The Mind and Voice are a Symphony,"
He replied.

We traveled far before I realized what He meant.

We approached a hilltop overlooking The City of White.

"Decisions turned to nothing,
and Our Eyes tell all we meant.

It's all that is left of Beauty, and they destroyed it."

I looked down to the hill to see It soaked with blood.

"I gave them All anyone could ask for, and all I could do is sit back and watch It, watching them destroy It!"

"Years ago, there was a Secret I had not accounted for, One for which The Answer only I held.

It was
The Connection of
All Unity.

They juggled worship. They built congregation to try to accentuate what they called my WORD and WONDER.

But, not one of them had the Wisdom to behold The Truth."

"What is The Truth???"

He handed me the same pipe as before, and in it laid three single Red feathers.

I took the pipe and consumed The Wisdom it had to offer.

Upon it I Understood. Understanding blankets me like a cool Brook.

> And, as His Lips remained still,
> His Words Echoed From Within.

> "They all forgot of
> the Symphony of the Soul!

In the beginning, they did take wonder at what's around them.

Gradually, they began to take advantage of what beheld them, established free will, and constructed shelter from what I had to offer.

Eventually, their eyes and Mind grew immunity of my Beauty.

They became unappreciative and greedy for the establishment, claiming ownership contained within My Creation.

> Segregation took place.

They felt the need to start to destroy it for their own independent creation.

THEY ESTABLISHED THEIR OWN ORDER!!

Blood was shed over My Beautiful Soil over
the privilege to even endure it.

As my upbringing fell to fallen Dreams,
They tried establishing
an embellishment of repent."

They began to build churches to separate themselves from each other in some sort of twisted unity of arrogant pride and vanity of belief!

Soon fell upon this war a small bird. I tried to contribute to the land's Salvation.

Upon its flesh are vibrant RED FEATHERS containing the simple relief in the embellishing perception altering Appreciation of WHAT Is with the Powerful WISDOM OF TRUTH."

"What is THE TRUTH?"

"THIS IS THEIR CHURCH!!"

This is their Heaven, Their Tranquility, their contemplation of what is overlooked, and they've DESTROYED IT!"

They would spend every moment obsessing over words of the past!

They embellished the Thought of EVERLASTING LIFE in ETERNITY.

They would wait their whole lives to behold what is behind and Beyond their dying day, weaving through ETERNITY as a reward for their Salvation.

THIS IS IT!

They're just too blind to see it!!

Every day they would pray for Salvation to me, closing their eyes to all I had to offer!!!

Someone other than I once said,

'They anticipate EVERLASTING LIFE, but don't know what to do on a rainy day.'

If they just opened Their Eyes, with a Single Breath, they would realize that THIS IS THE MEANING FOR THE ENTIRE CREATION...

THEIR ENJOYMENT!!"

"Then would be given their EVERLASTING LIFE,
UPON OBSERVANT TRANQUILITY.

They fought, slaughtered, all for this simple TRUTH, killing innocence over altered opinion.

All their blood was shed on These Hills as a result and greed of the WISDOM.

These simple feathers were all that remained.

They destroyed each other with fear, guilt, and greed.

You Are My Only.

You Are All That Is left upon a new attempt.

You Are All That Is left of The End.

And, Hopefully, You Will Be The New Beginning."

"Why me?"

"Because, you had The Eyes and the ability to endure all I have given you.

> You Are The Remaining Drop of Purity,
> and Now, With You,
> I Shall Begin Again,
> because You Hold The Ability to Deserve
> These Skies."

The Creator once again focused into my wandering Eyes.

His Eyes Becoming Endless Tunnels, Watch as I fall into an Endless Pit of Color, as swirling Calm grasps My Pulse.

And, Within a New Mind, as His Voice slowly fades into a crescendo with the ease of a Sunset,

The Wind calls in a longing desperation.

The crisp leaves crackle upon broken Silence.

I am trembling.

I am trembling to know I am Part of EXISTENCE.

I am Energy.

I am time.

Wisdom is never new, but simply revealed.

I am crackling leaves.

Every moment is but the same moment. We gauge the distance of moments through a proximate frame of reference, a fictitious measure of waiting. Days fade more rapidly as we reach the Autumn of Our Years. Time seems to change, rapidly acceding in pace.

But, I understand now, time is not changing; it is *I* that am changing.

I change time, because I *am* time.

I may increase its pace with my Heartbeat, or stretch a moment to the far edges of comprehension.

A moment may become Infinite,
as Infinity becomes an instant.

Time blankets the dawn
as the evening gently sleeps.

Internal Warmth illuminated every molecule
surrounding me as I saw my Self in EVERYTHING.

In The Beginning All Was, As It Is, and Was in The End. My Beginning, as Yours, shares the same moment as Our

Deaths, as with every Death, every Birth, and every Breath: Within The Same Moment.

All Is The Moment of This, or Was, or is Now, Infinitely Now.

This has been said.

This has been Lived.

You have already Lived every moment, yet to be Born.

Within this moment, within the moment of our Birth, the moment of Our Death, and our every Breath, We have already dispersed into the very Energy surrounding You, Within You, and moving every molecule.

But, because time does not exist, We have the privilege to be in the presence of the very Energy we soon will become.

And, because time does not exist, 'soon will' does not exist.

Hence, The Creator, Time, Energy, and We are The Same, Are One.

I Smiled, Feeling The Dawn as Eternity whispered a Truth as delicate as The Wind. I watched and felt every moment at once. In Peaceful Acceptance of Uncertainty, I confide in the Comfort of the moment that stretched Infinitely.

> I feel the dawn.
> I am the dawn.

I Suddenly Became The One I Seek.

I Realized This Place, This Brook, This Paradise That Was and Is This Endless Mural of Respect was not contained within the RED FEATHERS I have consumed, but Within My Self.

All the RED FEATHERS simply did was distract me from whatever it was that was detracting Me from This Unfathomable Beauty Surrounding Me, and The Joy Within Me.

This very Love, This Beauty, Joy, and Peace, Being Their Own Entity, are the only things remaining uncreated: Forever Present.

This Joy, This Peace, Unfathomably Present, is no longer a Glimpse or a Dream, but a New World that was and Is Forever Present.

They, This Brook, and We are ONE.

I Am The ONE, and The Very Place I Am seeking is not Self-contained,

but a SYMBIOTIC PARADISE.

It is misleading to have an End, because there are no Ends, and only when you Realize You Are time, do You Become Infinitely Patient.

BOOK THREE

BECOMING PEACE:
A Guidebook

Thoughts are *just* Thoughts and words are *just* words; both are extraneous to this FEELING[1]! I will not say this FEELING, because We are not tapped in to it this very moment. Granted, It's there. Thoughts are just so overwhelming sometimes!

I will save You and My Future Self the wasted Breath and ENERGY of comprehending extraneous words, because all suffering is temporary.

All suffering is temporary, but inevitable in this LIFE. At least We understand that suffering is but a creation of the Mind or an inevitable condition of this Earth.

> The only fruit of confusion is pain.[2]
> The only fruit of fear is pain.[3]

> The Mind is extraneous to FEELING.
> The Acceptance of suffering is The Beginning of ENLIGHTENMENT.[4]

On a quantum level, the only thing that makes Things As They Are, Reality, is ENERGY.

The Only thing that *We* Are is the ENERGY that we use for Thought or action.

> ENERGY cannot be destroyed,
> only transformed.

It is up to *Us* to decide where It goes.

---

[1] Every word capitalized is a Portal to GOD.
[2] Maharaji
[3] Maharaji
[4] Buddha

Energy Is All Around Us in Reality, and can't go anywhere, because It *Is* Reality; just take It in!

The only thing that is keeping us from Feeling This Connection With Reality is Our Minds!

What would you rather be a part of:

> The brain or the *Universe!?*

When We Can Completely Relax Our Minds, We Will Feel This Connection, share it, and become rewarded for Feeling It and sharing it!

> When We control Our Minds,
> We Become One With The Universe.

Our Minds will control us if we rely on things of this Earth and the uncontrolled Mind to get to the
> Hidden City of Enlightenment Within You.

As long as we as human kind continue take the devil's hand (things of this Earth and the uncontrolled Mind) to become enlightened, we will never be in <u>complete</u> control of Our Minds. Lack of *complete* control of Our Minds will not only cause us to fall, and we will fall, either to not having complete control of our Minds, which is theoretical insanity, or simply Death.

You will fall to a Death, either to Self-destruction in the deterioration of health at the ultimate level, or Death to Self-termination as a result of feeling the familiar infinite despair in complete consumption, pulling you to take your own Life.

That familiar infinite despair is rooted by a FEELING of inadequately that is derived from the pathological guilt that is created by our subconscious awareness that we lack *complete* emotional and mental control of ourselves.

The FEELING of inadequately is derived from the pathological guilt created by our subconscious self-awareness and our Mind's attempt to rationalize it is the only thing keeping us from the unfathomable FEELING of PEACE.

The Presence of That FEELING is GOD.

The simplicity of evil can be categorized into three rationalities.

A DEMON[5] is nothing less than an *uncontrolled Thought*,

A SIN[6] is nothing more than the very instant one loses the *complete* control of one's Thoughts and Emotions, or Feelings,

and, the devil is the uncontrolled Mind.

The Reality of evil is as simple as that, limited to the Mind, but the Power of the Ego and The Creativity of Imagination without Compassion is constantly robbing Us from realizing this simplicity through doubt or the exaggeration of Thought.

GOD Is The Unfathomably Good FEELING of PEACE, and the quantum and relative ENERGY that *is* Reality, Binding All Matter.

---

[5] Over- translation has caused the concept of demons to be an object of imagery instead of its allegorical purpose from the beginning of scripture.

[6] Sin is one of the most overanalyzed concepts in modern day religion. The obsession of uncertainty has been the root of many wars and tribulations.

Our True Self is the MIND's expression of THAT GOOD FEELING.

Our True Self is obtained by: completely relaxing the Mind, which is only possible *without* mental stimulation, accepting all Thoughts as simply Thoughts, and focusing on FEELING.

When That Good FEELING Is reached, It EMULATES *through* the Mind, which filters <u>all</u> extraneous Thought.

That EMULATION Is proved by the expressions and mannerisms of the host of the other party in the SPIRITUAL Communion of conversation.

You see as they ask themselves, 'Why does this person make me FEEL this way?' That expression lets you Know, 'They're FEELING This! This Is Real!' This is most apparent in the opposite sex.

This Is The Process that has, since the Beginning of ENLIGHTENMENT, been tagged with the word LOVE, but LOVE is just a word.

It Is a <u>FEELING</u> that allows you to KNOW It Is Real.

It Is a FEELING that allows you to KNOW What Is *Real*.

It Is a FEELING that allows you to KNOW What Is *Right*.

It Is a FEELING That Allows You to <u>*KNOW*</u>.

That FEELING Is there, Always There, You just have to cut out the Middle Man that is the uncontrolled Mind, the obsession to and of Thought, and the Ego to get to It.

At that moment, you will no longer have any questions, Only ANSWERS.

<u>These Are The KEYS to The Hidden City.</u>

At this moment, I hesitate using Mind expanding drugs even once more, because the last time I did so, granted gave me ENLIGHTENMENT in the form of self-awareness of Thought, but was too close to Hell.

Hell is but simply being trapped on this Earth or within your Mind with the FEELING of misery brought through FEELING the altered Perception that time is insignificant, inconstant, and without MEANING…

While within the same moment, lacking the FEELING that allows you to <u>*KNOW*</u>, filter Thought, and obtain PEACE.

It was too close to Hell, because it removed the <u>FEELING</u> of Knowledge and Certainty (which is GOD), leaving the vast presence of unfiltered Knowledge.

The vast awareness of Knowledge without the FEELING of Guidance to filter extraneous Thought *is* insanity, *is* Hell, and *is* the devil itself. The only way to rise above Hell is LOVE.

The Mind is a very delicate thing. When it is expanded or altered, it is as if you are walking on a wide road. On the left of this wide road, you see the City of ENLIGHTENMENT, and far on the right lay the City of Insanity.

As the Mind continues to be altered and expanded, that road becomes a narrow path, until finally comes the moment when the path suddenly becomes a tightrope upon which you are carefully maintaining balance between Both Cities.

You Feel and Know deep within you that moment on the tightrope, that if the Mind were to be altered even once more, it would be like a fierce gust of Wind hurling you into either City. A powerful presence of fear and uncertainty forces you to question which City you will fall in.

Be honest to Your Self.

Uncontrolled Thought has a feeling. You can sense this feeling in others and yourself. This is sensing demons.

The reason drugs have had such a powerful effect on human kind is because under their influence, they reveal to us The Reality and Presence of Heaven and Hell on this Earth and within ourselves is co-existent!

Complete Self-awareness of our subconscious is also revealed, containing both the uncontrolled presence and obsession of uncontrolled Thoughts without Peace (demons) and their overwhelming influence over Our Reality, as well as our chosen consciousness and intuition competing for Perception and expression.

But, the creation and allowance of this invasion of control is a subconscious choice! Drugs give complete self-control over the Mind with the forced awareness of losing it under their influence.

Losing Complete Self Control of the Mind is nothing to fear, nor is Thought, because the very desire for detachment from Our Minds is the essence of our humanity.

Though, for *Complete* Self Awareness, One must learn The Art of Detachment through Meditation and Patience.

Granted our Thoughts are *our* reality, but only when We Are In Complete Control of *our* reality do We Become Reciprocal to True Reality.

When uncontrolled Thoughts, or demons, are prevented through discipline and Meditation, then occurs True enlightenment, or Our Mind's Expression of Peace,

filtering all extraneous Thought!

As The Process of enlightenment proceeds, You Realize the True meaning of every lesson Life has ever taught You, the relevance or irrelevance of every word ever spoken to You, and You suddenly become Aware of the Purpose and Meaning of the Serendipity Within All Life.

The Path to Infinite Peace Is to be independent of all pleasures of all this Earth[7], but Reciprocal to the Gifts Within Us, and All Around Us.

As stated in the preface, the difference between Knowledge and Wisdom is that Wisdom is the overwhelming Presence of Feeling and Knowledge simultaneously. Without Feeling, Knowledge is just another book on a shelf, the product of Ego, things that don't need to be said.

<u>All</u> words, actions, and decisions are the Mind's expression of Emotion or concept.

---

[7] 'Independent of all pleasures of this Earth' does not imply necessarily to be completely without them, which I will come back to later, but to become stronger than them, freeing yourself from 'the need' that comes from physical and psychological dependency. This can only be possible through the discipline of cleansing the body of all Mind-altering substance for a period of time overcoming the transformation of your body's chemistry.

Feeling alters Thought, and Thought alters Feeling.
By controlling Thought, you thus control Feeling.

The root of all addictions ever faced is the feeling of detachment jaded with the excess of Thought in desperation to find the Peace kept to them by thinking.

<u>*All dependency to Earthly pleasure is the denial of suffering!*</u>

Earthly pleasure is useful to rise above the conditions of this Earth and the conditions of Our Mind, but excess of this *simple* solution takes its toll, and can turn to Hell.

Suffering must be accepted!!

We are all of different Minds, but have the same Soul!

The ability to choose Thought or action
is what makes us unique;

The ability to feel makes us ***One***.

The only Thoughts you should Trust are the
ones that come Through Peace.

With Peace With You, being lost is impossible, because where ever You Are Is The Place To Be. Because Peace Is Our Purpose for Being, why else wander?

Fear calls fear,
and though fear also calls compassion,
because the only fruit of fear is pain,
pain leads to envy,
envy leads to jealously,
jealousy leads to hate,

and hate leads to Death.

All ungodly Thoughts and actions of mankind are just their expression of what they are FEELING as a result of their demons robbing them of their PEACE.

It's not their fault!!

I *must* find PEACE within my Self – **Always.**

Confusion is the moment the Mind, or Ego, takes over the SOUL.

When confusion is FELT, it is important to Center Your (and Our) Self and Find (and Know) Peace; this is important because through the EMULATION of Emotion and Empathy, You Can FEEL the confusion of those you are communicating with as They Can Feel You.

> Thought and PEACE conceived a Child,
> and *We* Are That Child…

…and by *We*, I mean mankind.

Our Minds are like a bully, not to be trusted, that has been picking on Us from the moment We Were Born, but Now, Through SPIRITUALLY Conditioning Our SOUL, We Become strong enough that *We* Are in control.

The Purpose for Our every Thought and word is to craft a Message of PEACE. The only purpose for our actions is to bring PEACE where It is needed.

> We do not even need to speak.

If we simply *Become* the PEACE We would like to see in the world, Our Very Presence will allow The Minds of the confused, conflicted, and troubled to change, giving them the ability to change their Thoughts and FEEL with the ENERGY We Create With Our SOULS.

> We must slow down Our Thoughts,
> slow down our words…
> or you will briefly give PEACE and then
> take It away with our Ego.

> We Are All Each Other's Balance.
> Balance Is Guidance.

We get upset when people speak while we are speaking because of the Intuition that if they are speaking, they are thinking, if they are thinking; they are not Listening.

Listening is a form of Natural detachment.

Find the PASSION in all.

Find the CONNECTIONS in *Everything*.

You have nothing to prove and nothing to hide.

> Your Intuition will be able to Sense what
> TRUTH they are ready to have revealed.

The selfish obsession to one's own abilities and the effort to reveal them out of pride will only ultimately bring pain and confusion to others. Their confusion becomes your confusion, as you become tied up in the paradoxes of your own words.

The obsession to confusion, or the obsession to the fear of confusion can result in becoming a slave to the Ego, completely enthralled in the hopeless uncontrolled Mind, The devil.

Through the process of worshiping confusion, or meaningless Knowledge without PEACE, one becomes the devil through encouraging intelligent confusion and contagious emptiness.

Because LOVE reigns over all, the devil's control is only as temporary as the absence of LOVE, Which Reigns Over All, because…

LOVE *Is* The *Essence* of BEING.

The tolls for becoming the devil, which is temporary and is human, are serendipitous misery, overwhelming mental limitation, and the absence of FEELING.

PEACE is the only thing strong enough to Answer the questions of the UNIVERSE, not the Mind.

The Mind's conception of all great and WISE things is only but the result of PEACE's EMULATION through the Mind's reserve of all serendipitously learned WISDOM.

The concept of 'easy' and 'hard' is but the Mind's obsession with categorizing limitations subjectively instead of overcoming them.

All difficulty is relative.

I Am What I Am, and You Are What You Are.

We are What We Are, and The Lord is The Lord.

The Lord is Love and Is All There Is,

Infinitely Present.

The Ego denies the limits of Our Mind instead of accepting them.

Becoming thirsty with ignorance, the frustrating quest for answers through Earthly pleasures and suffering is inevitable. Accepting the Mind's limitations instead of denying them makes Life something of Wonder instead of frustration.

The Acceptance of Reality Makes Us Reciprocal to The UNIVERSE, instead of parasitical.

By keeping One's Self from PEACE through uncontrolled Thought, just your presence keeps PEACE form those around you, because they FEEL you.

People can FEEL the fears of others as easily as they can FEEL PEACE through the SPIRITUAL Communion of conversation and of Your (and Our) Presence.

Your fears are their fears, as their fears are yours.
You FEEL them, as they FEEL you.

That is why Peace is such a responsibility.

We don't even have to speak to help others change. Just by bringing PEACE to One's Self in their presence brings them PEACE, not to mention Guidance through example, because the Strength of Our PEACE and The Way You allow them to FEEL *forces* their Thoughts to change.

Feeling Peace is a more Powerful Form of

The Truth

Spiritual Communion than speaking it.

A Message of Complete Peace and liberation from Our Mind is Our Purpose for Living, and the time has come to rid the Earth of all demons.

Do not let your Mind mislead you; you will FEEL what is Right, True, Good, and Real.

If words and Thoughts still continue to keep anyone from Enlightenment, you must blow their Mind to free them from it. This may hurt them at first, but it is not You causing their pain, but their Mind's retaliation to maintain dominance over their being by limiting conception.

We all make mistakes; we are human.

Life is mistakes, Perfect Mistakes.

We must Live Life in the paradox of Accepting them and avoiding them at the same time.

Though confusion is only the FEELING of the Ego taking control of the Soul, or limiting conception, the Ego can be strong enough to comprehend on an excelled level of Knowledge without confusion. This is limited through the lack of FEELING, limiting the FEELING of meaning, leaving emptiness only pride can fill.

Sometimes pride seems worthy of accomplishment, but unless the accomplishment is selfless, one becomes vulnerable to intelligent confusion and contagious emptiness.

If you are leading others to obsess over the path of meaningless Knowledge, manipulating their thirst for

UNDERSTANDING with false Hopes and pointless concepts in an intelligent fashion, whether it is understood or oblivious to them, you *are* the devil, and *will fall*.

Though Thought and EMOTION is the Essence of Being, when the two become a personal obsession of identity to please, impress, or compare yourself to others, one must admit to One's Self this is the subtle product of the Ego instead of Complete PEACE.

If Thoughts and EMOTIONS are still controlled by outside validation instead of the Pure Intention of Bringing PEACE, there is still present a subconscious selfishness.

We must become selfless.

As the greatest feat of the ultimate warrior is to lay down his sword when given the chance to slay his greatest foe…

…as is the Greatest Feat of The Ultimate Thinker
to lay Their Thoughts down to PEACE.

When we let fear, anger, hate, doubt, and confusion (all element of the Mind) take control of our FEELINGS, Our SOUL has become temporarily taken, making us vulnerable to Hell.

<u>*Know Hell (insanity) is impossible through
The Presence of Unconditional Love!!*</u>

Rise above the conditions of this Earth through health and Meditation first before mental stimulation, and your Mind's obsession will become PEACE, not suffering.

The Truth

Though always remember, over activity of the Mind robs us of our patience, making us a slave to time.

When you are a slave to time, it limits you from Peace, making you a slave to the Mind in search of it!

The concept of Time is a creation of the Mind for measurement, but is only relative and subjective.

The Mind can play many tricks to try to create Hell.

Hell is only one side of a duel universe.

The implication of 'duel universe' is that every Thought has simultaneously presented within it The Infinite Presence of Perspectives it can be seen from, winding to become two simultaneous sides of the Ultimate Truth.

The two sides are:
The Light and **The Dark Side**,

which are the same as the The Blue and The Red.

This is true within every Thought.

That is why the Mind is not to be trusted, because without an Enlightened sense of intuition, and because we are human,we are unable to decipher the Light from **The Dark Side**.

That is why we can only trust Feeling!

When we Trust Feeling Completely, We Trust God Completely, and Will Love and Understand All of The Colors at Once.

The Love and Presence of All and Every Color at Once Is

The City of White and Is God Consciousness.

We know Hell.
We are aware how to rise above it.
We are now Wise enough to refuse to go back!!
Demons are only Thoughts.

We Can <u>Choose</u> not to create them.
I know the devil too well to become its fool!!!

We Are The Energy Share for Thought,
Experience, and Feeling.

If We Choose to lose all identity,
and Choose to Become selfless,
and make Our every Thought, Experience, and Feeling
Peace, The True Self,

We *Are* Peace.

If We *Are* Peace,
We *Are* Love.

If We *Are* Love,
I We Will Find Strength.
We *Are* Strength!

You and I *are* Christ, The Ultimate Form of Evolution, until the moment we allow demons (uncontrolled thoughts) to govern and control Minds. Demons are only uncontrolled Thoughts, and can be made non-existent by controlling every Thought Through Peace and teaching others to do the same.

The Truth

Only when Our Mind Is Completely At Rest, Completely At Peace: Pure, will We All Hear the Voice of God Within Us, Between Us, and All Around Us, Spiraling To and Through Infinity Infinitely.

We can fall. W can suffer.
We are human. That can be Life.

Because we are human,
We can fall, and We can rise.
If We fall, it is Our Choice.

We will destroy "evil," or what we
Know is the "less magnificent,"
because We Choose to Become The Light!

Though, In Truth, We Will destroy nothing,
Nor will we need to.

Destruction and the intention to destroy will be a seed of its own destruction to those who desire and intend to destroy.

Thus, Those Who Love and Know They *Are* Love Will Be Protected With and By Their Love As A Shield, and the Collective Will Be Rebalanced and Healed to Reign With Life and Love With and Within Paradise.

When a Being comes to the pivotal time of the development of Their conscious and subconscious Mind, or Id and Self, becoming completely selfless without identity thus leaving a Naturally Creative Identity, They comes to the overwhelming task of complete subconscious awareness when God and the devil are literally fighting with all their might for your Soul.

This extreme consciousness is the tightrope or the thin line between the BEAUTIFUL City of ENLIGHTENMENT and the terrifying City of Insanity.

That line becomes so thin,
BALANCE is completely necessary.
LOVE IS That BALANCE.

The Mind is too powerful,
only to be used, not trusted.
There is DIVINE GRACE in knowing every mistake you have ever made was not entirely your fault.

There is the ULTIMATE REVELATION at the end of suffering, Life's greatest lesson to remember...

<u>YOU AND I ARE CHRIST.</u>

It also takes choosing to become the devil so many times to realize, we have always chosen.

We have always chosen to suffer,
chosen confusion,
chosen worry,
chosen fear,
chosen to become the devil.

This Revelation, because of the Reciprocity of sharing FEELING with Others, is both the Ultimate Gift, the ultimate curse, and the ultimate struggle...

...Choice.

WE, LOVE, CHRIST, TRUTH, JOY, HOPE, LIFE and ARE **ONE** always in all ways, and will continue to be so consciously until the moment we let the devil (the uncontrolled Mind) win, but because Love Reigns Over All…

it won't.

When comprehension seems an obstacle through doubt, One must ask One's Self, 'What is the purpose for this doubt I am holding on to? Am I choosing *it* or is *it* choosing me?'

Only the *Mind* is confusing, and shouldn't be trusted…

Free your Mind and follow your Soul.

<u>*The thin line, the tightrope, between Enlightenment and Insanity is FEELING!!*</u>

The Truth is *not* a concept,
It is a feeling!

The Truth is the same feeling *that is God*,
God is the same feeling *that is Peace!*
God <u>is</u> Peace, Us, Love, Christ, Truth, Joy,
Hope, and LIFE.

Life is every breath,
hence God is every breath.

One only Breathes as long as Hope,
or the subconscious quest for The Truth,
Is Within Them.

Within the last six minutes of brain activity, when the body dies and the brain remains active, the brain releases DMT, a naturally produced hallucinogenic entity that is released only within the first moment of Birth and the last moments of Death.

Within these last six minutes, consciousness becomes Infinite, complying with the theory of Relativity.

Deep within consciousness and Infinite landscape of the quantum time within the UNIVERSE within Our Minds emerges THE ULTIMATE CONSCIOUSNESS.

THE ULTIMATE CONSCIOUSNESS is subconscious' finite perception of chaos, fear, hate, doubt, misery, and darkness (with the temporary absence of PEACE, US, LOVE, CHRIST, TRUTH, JOY, HOPE, AND LIFE), WHICH is Hell, but a theoretically finite Hell, lasting only the last six minutes the brain remains active, and ends with the emergence into Infinite Consciousness.

The Infinite Consciousness is the subconscious' complete and Infinite perception of PEACE, LOVE, TRUTH, HOPE, LIFE and BEAUTY,

which *is* GOD, *IS* HEAVEN,

AND *is* INFINITE and EVERLASTING LIFE.

The Answer Has Always Been You.

Made in the USA
San Bernardino, CA
21 December 2017